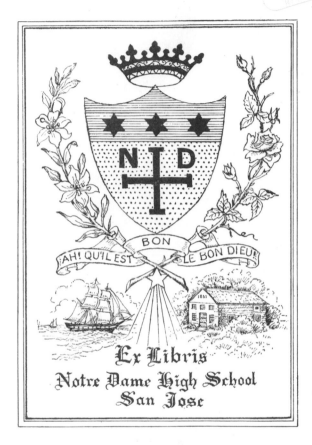

Ex Libris
Notre Dame High School
San Jose

## THE PURCHASE OF ALASKA

In 1860, William H. Seward, as a United States senator from New York, stated in a speech at St. Paul, Minnesota:

> *Standing here and looking far off into the Northwest, I see the Russian, as he busily occupies himself in establishing seaports and towns and fortifications on the verge of this continent, as the outposts of St. Petersburg; and I can say: "Go on, and build your outposts all along the coast, up even to the Arctic Ocean; they will yet become the outposts of my country,—monuments of the civilization of the United States in the Northwest."*

In 1867, William H. Seward, as secretary of state under President Andrew Johnson, signed the treaty with Russia for the cession of Alaska.


## PRINCIPALS

WILLIAM H. SEWARD, American secretary of state, who negotiated the purchase of Alaska in 1867.

EDOUARD DE STOECKL, Russian foreign minister in America, who contracted the treaty that ceded Alaska to the United States.

CHARLES SUMNER, Senator and chairman of the Senate Foreign Relations Committee, whose prestige and powerful oratory on behalf of the sale of Alaska helped ratify the treaty in the Senate.

ROBERT KENNICOTT, Major and chief of explorations with the Collins Overland Telegraph Company.

HENRY M. BANNISTER, Assistant to Kennicott, sent by the Smithsonian Institution to Alaska.

ALEXANDER GORCHAKOV, Foreign minister of Russia.

ALEXANDER II, Czar of Russia.

GRAND DUKE CONSTANTINE, Brother of Alexander II.

SPENCER FULLERTON BAIRD, Assistant secretary of the Smithsonian Institution.

A FOCUS BOOK

# The Purchase of Alaska,

## March 30, 1867

### *A Bargain at Two Cents an Acre*

### by Peter Sgroi

FRANKLIN WATTS | NEW YORK | LONDON

Photographs courtesy of: Alaska Historical Library—
pp. 26–27; Alaska Travel Division—p. 51; Library of
Congress—pp. vi, 6, 9, 15, 18, 21, 28, 33, 42, 44, 52, 57;
Tundra Times—p. 60; University of Alaska Archives
—pp. 36, 39; Washington Convention and Visitors
Bureau—p. 48.

Title page photograph courtesy of University of Alaska
Archives—the Alaskan wilderness on the Yukon River

Cover by Ginger Giles
Map by George Buctel

Library of Congress Cataloging in Publication Data

Sgroi, Peter P
    The purchase of Alaska, March 30, 1867.

    (A Focus book)
    Bibliography: p.
    Includes index.
    SUMMARY: An account of the purchase of Alaska
by the United States from Russia in 1867.
    1. Alaska—Annexation—Juvenile literature.
[1. Alaska—Annexation]  I. Giles, Ginger, ill.
II. Buctel, George, ill.  III. Title.
E669.S46         979.8'02         74-26677
ISBN 0-531-01089-9

# Contents

# Russia Wants
# to Sell

On December 12, 1866, Alexander II, czar of Russia, became a very worried man. He received a special dispatch from his foreign minister, Alexander Gorchakov, concerning trouble over his Alaskan colony, then called Russian America. The emperor always seemed to be troubled over this huge possession—586,400 square miles at the top of the North American continent. He was reminded daily of the financial decline of the territory. Stocks in the Russian American Company were tumbling. Stock worth about 500 rubles (then $372) not long before could not find buyers at 25 rubles ($55). Alexander's royal commission had reported earlier that the colony was not worth more than $4.4 million and that he should dispose of it immediately.

On another occasion, reports from the czar's foreign minister in America caused him to be uneasy—every day more and more Americans were settling in the Oregon Territory and were resentful that they were excluded from any trade benefits in the Russian possession. Russian Foreign Minister Edouard de Stoeckl recognized what happened when Americans became obsessed with the idea of "manifest destiny," and he so informed his emperor. Even Rear-Admiral Papov had told the czar of the great misery and harm that the Russian American Company had brought to the territory, to the natives, and to the commerce of

*Valuable as the territory might have*
*been, Alaska gave Alexander II*
*an almost constant headache*

Alaska. All the company thought of was dividends, complained the admiral.

But perhaps this new dispatch, however worrisome, would solve the czar's problem. He read it again and then considered the last part of the message. The best solution to the problem was to sell this liability, the communication stated, and it suggested calling a special meeting of Russia's ministers to discuss the question. The dispatch was signed by Michael Reutern, minister of finance; Edouard de Stoeckl; and the Grand Duke Constantine, the czar's brother.

Why not? Alexander thought. Then he would be rid of this nagging problem. So he called an emergency meeting of ministers at the palace. Within four days and after much discussion, they agreed, on December 16, 1866, to sell the huge and troublesome territory of Alaska to the United States.

# The Logical
# Customer

Russia's choice of a buyer for Alaska was in part based on the realization of what happened to Americans when they attempted to carry out plans for continental expansion. The Russians had become concerned by this American threat, as evidenced in the following communications.

From the Russian foreign minister to Count Karl Nesselrode, minister of foreign affairs, in January, 1856:

> *The establishment of Americans in the neighborhood of our possessions north west, shall place these ultimately in actual danger and shall become a source of embarrassment and of vexation between the two governments.*

In a letter to Foreign Minister Gorchakov, dated Washington, December 2, 1857, de Stoeckl reported a conversation with American President James Buchanan:

> *In great alarm, he sought an interview with President Buchanan to ascertain the truth or falsity of these reports, asking whether the Mormons were coming as colonists or conquerors. Buchanan laughingly replied that he knew nothing of the destination of the polygamists, and it mattered little to him provided he got rid of them.*

The situation made quite an impression on the emperor, and in the margin of the ambassador's report, he wrote: "That comes to the support of the idea of settling, right now, the question of our American possessions."

But perhaps the greatest concern over America's actions

was stated in a report on the Russian colonies dated February 7, 1860. Its suspected author was Papov, who was at sea in the North Pacific about that time. The writer said:

> *It is easy enough for Europeans to sneer at the Monroe Doctrine and "Manifest Destiny," but if they were better acquainted with the Americans they would know that these ideas are in their very blood and in the air they breathe. There are twenty millions of Americans, every one of them a free man filled with the idea that America is for Americans. They have taken California, Oregon, and sooner or later they will get Alaska. It is inevitable. It cannot be prevented; and it would be better to yield with good grace and cede the territory to them. Let them have the Alaskan mainland, the Aleutians, the islands in the Bering Sea—geographically all these are American—but let us retain the Commander Islands so as not to have Yankees too near us. [The Commander—or Komandorskie—Islands in the southwest Bering Sea were retained by Russia.]*

The United States, therefore, was the logical customer for the purchase of Alaska. It was also fortunate that Americans and Russians were on very good terms at the time. In fact, the general atmosphere enveloping Russia and the United States at the close of the American Civil War could not have been more congenial for any kind of negotiations.

On the surface, friendship between the young democratic nation of the New World and the most autocratic country of the Old World might have seemed unlikely, but they actually had a number of ties. Both countries were huge, self-sufficient areas. Both tried to fuse different peoples. Both had insurrections during the 1860s. Both had almost simultaneously freed millions of subjugated peoples.

[4]

During the American Civil War, Russia had shown its friendship to the United States in many ways. When Napoleon III proposed that Europe intervene in the war, Russia opposed such a plan. Both Great Britain and France seemed hostile to the Union forces and likely to intervene on behalf of the Confederacy. To the Americans, it was Russia that thwarted the ambitions of Great Britain and France. (Russia was anti-British because it believed Great Britain was preventing the Russians from being the dominant influence in the Balkans, Constantinople, Afghanistan, and Persia.)

Then:

> *On September 24, 1863, two Russian warships appeared off New York City, joining the one already there and heralding the arrival of a fleet of some six vessels . . . On October 12, nearly three weeks after the initial surprise in New York, another Russian fleet of some six warships began to gather in San Francisco Bay. . . .*

Shortly before the Russian fleet arrived, a rumor began that the United States and Russia would soon conclude a mutual defense alliance. The rumor seemed confirmed with the arrival of the Russian ships. At the time the northern, or Union, forces were urgently in need of assistance, and the unexpected visit of the Russians seemed to highlight the fact that Alexander II was not only a friend but one prepared to fight on the side of friendship.

"God bless the Russians!" exclaimed Secretary of the Navy Gideon Wells, and that sentiment was echoed throughout the land. Even though the fleets were small and the ships old and unseaworthy, the visiting Russians were almost hysterically overwhelmed with entertainment. Delegations from various northern states arrived in New York to pay their respects, and

[5]

*The Russian fleet in
San Francisco Bay
during the Civil War*

the New York Central Railroad arranged to take a party of Russian officers to Niagara Falls. When the fleet visited Washington and Boston, the guests were wined and dined expensively. Elaborate balls were held, and the names of Abraham Lincoln and Alexander II were much extolled.

So what Czar Alexander II said in 1866 was basically true: "The Russian and American people have no injuries to forget or remember." The United States was the logical purchaser of Alaska. It was the one nation that could use Alaska most effectively to thwart the ambitions of Great Britain. Although regarded as a liability to the czar's government, Alaska would strengthen the United States hold on the Pacific. The transfer would then place British Columbia between American territory on both the north and the south. Any resulting unpleasantness between the United States and Great Britain would be greatly advantageous to the interests of Russia.

# Earlier Attempts

The 1866 decision was undoubtedly the most formidable move to date toward the sale of Alaska. However, it climaxed a series of intermittent, premature attempts on behalf of the United States to buy the territory.

The earliest, somewhat superficial, mention of a possible purchase was contained in a letter published in the *Washington Daily Morning Chronicle* on January 28, 1845. It was written to President James Polk by his newly appointed secretary of the treasury, Robert J. Walker. In the letter, Walker stated:

> *Our just and rightful claim to the whole Oregon will, I trust, be successfully asserted by you. This would leave no European power upon our Pacific Coast except Russia, whose well-known friendship to us would, it is hoped, induce her to cede to us her North American Territory.*

A devised, "fictitious sale" of Alaska to a San Francisco concern in 1854 did not place any new possession in American hands, but it did plant the idea of a transfer in the American mind. The incident occurred when a possible war between Russia and Britain brought about an ingenious scheme to save the Russian possession. Britain's navy could easily seize Alaska, so

*In a letter to President James Polk (left) in 1845, some mention was made of a possible Alaskan sale Right: Senator William Gwin felt that Britain would see through the false contract to "sell" Alaska*

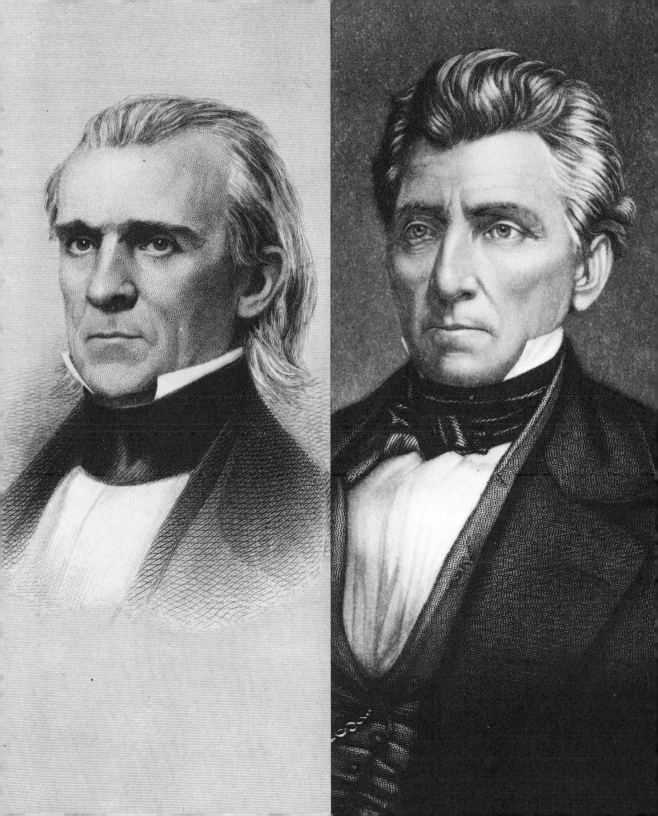

P. S. Kostromitinov, agent of the Russian American Company in San Francisco and also the Russian vice-consul there, devised the "sale" of the colony to the American Russian Commercial Company. The sale was presented by Lucien Herman, Commercial's vice-president. This fake deal even included sending a set of contracts to be approved in January, 1854, from California to the Russian delegation in Washington. The contracts left blank the spaces that pertained to the price and date of the transaction.

In Washington, the Russian foreign minister consulted William L. Marcy, the American secretary of state, and William M. Gwin, senator from California. Both Americans agreed that Britain would see through the false contract, and it should not be made public. That proved unnecessary, anyway, because Britain, through its Hudson Bay Company, agreed on March 23 to the neutralization of Russia's northwest possessions. In fact, the fake deal was dropped, but rumors of a possible sale persisted. Newspapers, working with circumstantial evidence, reported that Russia was financially bankrupt and that the czar was willing to sell Alaska at any price. Americans began to take the rumors as fact. So persistent was the gossip that even Marcy and Gwin, who knew of the false sale, approached de Stoeckl about a possible deal in 1856. The Russian minister assured them that the newspaper stories were false and that the czar had no desire to part with his American possessions.

The next move toward the purchase of Alaska began when de Stoeckl arrived in Washington from the Russian capital of St. Petersburg in 1859. While he was in Russia, it was agreed that should the United States again consider a possible purchase, the idea would be viewed more seriously. No sooner had de Stoeckl arrived in Washington than Gwin approached him on the matter.

*Throughout December 1859 the Senator, professing to speak for President Buchanan, had several interviews with Stoeckl in which he unofficially represented, "that Russia was too far off to make the most of these possessions, and that, as we are near, we can derive more from them." In reply to an inquiry from Stoeckl, he asserted that the United States would "go as high as $5,000,000 for the purchase."*

Believing that $5 million was a fair price for Alaska, de Stoeckl immediately reported the offer to St. Petersburg. But the Russian foreign office turned it down because Russia could see no political advantage in giving up the colony. However, the Russian minister to America was instructed to keep negotiations pending and to inform John Appleton, assistant secretary of state, and Senator Gwin that they would have to raise the price.

De Stoeckl knew that Appleton would soon leave office. Consequently, the Russian minister mentioned very little to him about the matter. However, de Stoeckl broached the subject of finances and had detailed discussions with Gwin about Alaska. The California senator assured de Stoeckl that the Pacific Coast representatives would be willing to offer a higher price. Gwin mentioned that, for the time being, negotiations were out of the question. The present Congress would not pass any measure that was recommended by the soon to be departing Buchanan cabinet, no matter how beneficial it was to the United States. Negotiations for Alaska could not be resumed until the new administration was in office.

On April 12, 1861, the South Carolinians opened fire on Fort Sumter and ushered in the American Civil War. As a result, the Lincoln administration was in no position to bargain with the Russian foreign office should an offer for Alaska have been forthcoming.

SUCTEL

CHUKCHI SEA

BEAUFORT SEA

RUSSIA

SIBERIA

Bering Strait

BROOKS RANGE

Colville R.

GREAT BEAR LAKE

SEWARD PENINSULA

Porcupine River

Peel River

Mackenzie River

Fort Yukon

N

Nulato

ST. LAWRENCE IS.

ALASKA

Yukon River

Yukon River

NORTHWESTERN TERRITORIES

Mt. McKinley +

ALASKA RANGE

NUNIVAK IS.

Kuskokwim R.

C A N A D A

BERING SEA

Cook Inlet

KENAI PEN.

BRITISH COLUMBIA

Bristol Bay

ALEUTIAN RANGE

Kodiak

KODIAK IS.

GULF OF ALASKA

Sitka

ALASKA PENINSULA

ALEUTIAN ISLANDS

Unalaska

PACIFIC        OCEAN

North Pole

ARCTIC        OCEAN

Arctic Circle

RUSSIA

SIBERIA

Amur R.

ALASKA

CANADA

BRITISH COLUMBIA

UNITED STATES

Puget Sound

ALEUTIAN ISLANDS

San Francisco

ALASKA

1867

PACIFIC        OCEAN

0    100    200    300    400

Miles

The war slowed down negotiations between the United States and Russia. A confidential letter, written on December 26, 1864, showed that it did not, however, completely end the matter. The letter was written to Cassius Marcellus Clay, American minister in Russia, and signed by William H. Seward, Lincoln's secretary of state. In it was an invitation that Clay was to extend to the Grand Duke Constantine, the foremost Russian champion of an Alaskan sale to the United States. Seward wished that "it were possible for him to come out and spend a few months in America. I think it could be beneficial to us and by no means unprofitable to Russia. I forbear from specifying my reasons."

Now, as a result of the 1866 meeting at the emperor's palace, Alexander II appointed de Stoeckl to go to Washington and try to get the government of the United States to purchase Alaska. De Stoeckl, a clever and astute diplomat, prepared in the spring of 1867 to meet with an overambitious and enthusiastic expansionist, William H. Seward.

# Negotiating a Treaty

As soon as de Stoeckl arrived in New York, he received an offer for the purchase of Alaska. It came, however, from an unexpected quarter, not from the American State Department—it was a private senatorial request. Senator Cornelius Cole of California tried to buy Alaska on behalf of some of his constituents!

Following his initial interview with de Stoeckl during the first week of March, Cole reported: "After full and free consultation with de Stoeckl, I regarded the matter as in effect settled in favor of the San Francisco Company, and I so informed them."

Nevertheless, Secretary Seward had begun negotiations for outright sale before Cole could get another interview. A friend is believed to have informed Seward that de Stoeckl was empowered to sell the territory.

In the next interview with Cole, de Stoeckl informed him of the new situation. The Russian minister expressed regret that he would be forced to disappoint the Californians. The senator decided not to object to ceding the territory to the United States government, and he stepped aside to give Seward a free hand.

The Russian minister called on Secretary of State Seward during the second week of March, 1867. In time-honored political fashion, the two statesmen avoided coming directly to the point. Seward opened the proceedings with a request on behalf

*Senator Cornelius Cole*
*wanted to buy Alaska for*
*some of his constituents*

of the citizens of Washington Territory, who desired permission to fish in Alaskan waters. It was only after this request was denied that the secretary of state inquired whether Russia would sell Alaska to the United States.

Now that de Stoeckl knew the United States was willing to bargain, the conversation proceeded more smoothly and rapidly. Both agreed that the sale would be advantageous for the two countries. They decided that before any official commitments be registered, Seward should speak to President Andrew Johnson, who had taken over the office on Lincoln's death in April, 1865. When they met again a day or two later, the secretary reported that the President was not enthusiastic about the purchase, but he was willing to leave the matter to the judgment of the cabinet.

*So, on March 15, Seward produced a draft of a treaty concession in a meeting of the Cabinet where all agreed as to the wisdom of acquiring the territory.*

In de Stoeckl's communication of March 18, he told Foreign Minister Gorchakov of his progress and included the information that he hoped to get $6 million or more for the sale. With that goal in mind, de Stoeckl met again with Seward shortly after the American was authorized by the cabinet to negotiate. Before any discussion of price, Seward had first to assure the Russian minister that the United States Senate would definitely ratify the pending treaty. The Russian minister at first desired to enlist personally the support of his friends in Congress. However, Seward did not want the initiative to come from the Capitol, and he convinced the Russian that it was an administrative measure that required secrecy. Now both were ready to discuss the price of the transfer.

Seward started the bidding at $5 million, but when he saw the cold look in de Stoeckl's face he raised it another $500,000. It was now de Stoeckl's turn. "After he finished shaking his head, the Russian demanded $10,000,000." The meeting produced no agreement.

During the week they met two or three times, and finally the haggling ended with the agreed price of $7 million for the territory of Alaska. But there were still two other less important although formidable obstacles. De Stoeckl was advised by cable to demand that the money be paid in London, and that the United States take over some obligations of the Russian American Company. The secretary of state would not accept those conditions.

Seward's refusal deadlocked negotiations until he attempted a compromise. On March 23, 1867, he wrote to the Russian delegation in Washington, D.C.:

*Mr. Seward to Mr. de Stoeckl*
*Department of State*
*Washington, March 23, 1867.*

*Sir:*
*With reference to the proposed convention between our respective governments for a cession by Russia of her American territory to the United States, I have the honor to acquaint you that I must insist upon that clause in the sixth article of the draught which declares the cession to be free and unencumbered by any reservations, privileges, franchises, grants, or possessions by any associated companies, whether corporate or incorporate, Russian or any other, ever, I will add two hundred thousand dollars to the consideration money on that account.*

*An engraving of the settlement
of Sitka, around the
time of the purchase of Alaska*

*I avail myself of the occasion to offer you a renewal assurance of my most distinguished consideration.*

*William H. Seward*

The Russian minister immediately condescended, as witnessed by his reply on March 25:

*Mr. de Stoeckl to Mr. Seward (Translation)*
*Imperial Legation of Russia to the United States*
*Washington, March 25, 1867*

*Mr. Secretary of State:*

*I have had the honor to receive the note which you were pleased to address to me on 23rd March, 1867, to inform me that the federal government insists that the clause inserted in article sixth of the project of convention must be strictly maintained, and that the territory to be ceded to the United States must be free from any engagement and privileges conceded either by the government or by companies.*

*In answer, I believe myself authorized, Mr. Secretary of State, to accede literally to this request on the conditions indicated in your note. Please accept, Mr. Secretary of State, the assurance of my very high consideration.*

*Stoeckl*

So a compromise was reached. Russia agreed to cede the territory "free and unencumbered by any reservations." The United States agreed to pay an additional $200,000 to make up for the loss in exchange.

William Seward realized that he must now act quickly to conclude negotiations before the adjournment of Congress. He therefore had de Stoeckl immediately send an outline of the proposed treaty to St. Petersburg over the newly laid and expensive Atlantic cable. The cable was sent on the same day Seward received the compromise note from the Russians, on March 25, and the United States paid the cost of it, which was $8,379.

De Stoeckl wired Gorchakov:

*Negotiations ended; result project of treaty follows:*

*Article 1: cession of our colonies, frontiers of territory ceded, on the east, line of demarcation of our treaty of 1825 with England, on the West exactly the line of demarcation sent me by the minister of the navy.*

*Article 2: property of the crown ceded to the United States, private property remains with individuals to whom it belongs, Orthodox churches remain sole property of persons of this creed with full liberty to exercise their religion.*

*Article 3: inhabitants of colonies can return to Russia or remain and enjoy all rights of American citizens.*

*Article 4: Russia will appoint one or two agents to make transfer to the United States of ceded territory.*

*Article 5: After exchange of ratifications of this treaty all fortifications, and military posts will be handed over to troops of the United States; Russian troops will retire as soon as possible and practical.*

*The two principal dealers for the sale and purchase of Alaska— William H. Seward, secretary of state of the United States, and Edouard de Stoeckl, Russian foreign minister in America*

*Article 6: United States shoulders no obligations contracted by our company.*

*Article 7: ratification to be exchanged at Washington.*

*I send this telegram at request of Seward who told me if I receive answer within six days treaty can be signed and confirmed by Senate next week. A simple authorization by telegraph to sign treaty will be equivalent to full power in due form.*

A reply from St. Petersburg came four days later, on March 29, 1867. It read: *"L'Empereur autorise vente pour sept millions de dollars, ainsi que signature de traité."* ("The emperor authorizes the sale for seven million dollars, as well as signature of treaty.")

Many historians contend that de Stoeckl made the following move after receiving the telegram.

*On the evening of March 29, 1867, Stoeckl called at Seward's home in Washington. He brought the welcome news that the Czar had given his consent to the transaction, and suggested that the treaty be concluded the next day at the State Department.*

It is well known that de Stoeckl personally brought the news to Seward. What is usually omitted, however, is the following note he sent before his visit:

*Mr. de Stoeckl to Mr. Seward (Translation)*
*Washington, March 29, 1867*

*Mr. Secretary of State:*

*I have the honor to inform you that by a telegram dated 29 of the month from St. Petersburg, Prince Gorchakov informs me that his Majesty the Emperor of all Russia gives his consent to the cession of the Russian possessions on the American continent to the United States for the stipulated sum of seven millions two hundred thousand dollars in gold, and that his Majesty the Emperor invests me with full powers to negotiate and sign the treaty.*

*Please accept, Mr. Secretary of State, the assurance of my very high consideration.*

*Stoeckl*

# The Signing

Seward accepted de Stoeckl's good news on Friday evening, March 29, at his home, but the secretary of state would not go along with the suggestion that the treaty be concluded the next day at the State Department. Not anxious to give up his customary Saturday night card game, he told de Stoeckl that the treaty should be concluded that very night.

Somewhat startled, de Stoeckl replied that the State Department was closed, but Seward assured him that if the Russian could get his delegation together before midnight, the department would be open and ready for business.

Seward asked his son Frederick, who was acting assistant secretary of state, to locate Charles Sumner, chairman of the Senate Committee on Foreign Relations. On that Friday, Sumner did not reach home until late in the evening. There he found a note from Seward asking him to go to the secretary's home. Sumner did so and was met by Seward's son. Both men joined de Stoeckl for the trip to the State Department, where the treaty was being copied.

The Russian minister realized his great political dependence on Sumner's future support in the Senate. Without his powerful oratory and prestige of office, the pending treaty could be doomed. It was no small wonder that, as they departed, the Russian turned to Sumner and said, "You will not fail us."

Secrecy prevailed over the whole transaction at the State Department. Little is known about the details of the signing of the treaty with Russia for the purchase of Alaska. A painting by Emanuel Leutze is the only record of the individuals who participated in the transaction. De Stoeckl and Ulademak Bodisco, his secretary of legation, were present, as were Seward and his son; R. S. Chew, chief clerk of the American delegation; and William Hunter, a French translator. (French was the customary language of diplomacy at the time.) Charles Sumner is also shown in the painting, but was not actually present at the signing.

At four o'clock on the morning of March 30, 1867, the treaty was put into formal form and signed. That was the last day of the current session of Congress. Therefore, only a few hours later the treaty for the purchase of Alaska was sent to the Senate by President Johnson. The next step was its reference to the Committee on Foreign Affairs.

On April 1, 1867, the Senate convened in executive session by proclamation of the President of the United States. The Committee on Foreign Relations proceeded to the consideration of the treaty. The committee consisted of Charles Sumner (chairman), William Fessenden of Maine, Donald Cameron of Pennsylvania, James Harlan of Iowa, Oliver Morton of Indiana, James Patterson of New Hampshire, and Reverdy Johnson of Maryland. The senators carefully considered the pros and the cons of the sale. Discussion of the issue, however, was not limited

Over: *the famous painting by Emanuel Leutze of the signing of the Alaska purchase, March 30, 1867. Shown left to right: chief clerk R. S. Chew; Secretary of State Seward; William Hunter, French translator; Ulademak Bodisco, Russian secretary of legation; Foreign Minister de Stoeckl; Senator Sumner (who was not actually present at the signing); and Frederick Seward, the secretary's son*

to this authorized body. At the same time, corresponding debates were carried on just outside the chamber of the Senate. Among the friendly influences exerted there was strong pressure from Thaddeus Stevens, acknowledged leader of the House of Representatives. Although he was without constitutional voice on the possible ratification of the treaty, he did not refrain from giving his earnest testimony.

The Alaskan treaty was reported by Sumner on April 8, 1867, without amendment, and with the recommendation that the Senate advise and consent thereto. The test of passage came the very next day. The treaty with Russia for the cession of Alaska was before the Senate on April 9, 1867. But chances for ratification were poor. The Alaskan treaty had come at a time when the Reconstruction controversy was shortly to climax in the impeachment trial of President Johnson. The senators regarded the treaty as an annoying interruption, and as an effort on the part of a tormented administration to cover its domestic wrongs with an amazing victory in the field of diplomacy. Seward was a target of the bitterness directed against his superior and also had accumulated a great many of his own personal enemies. Many senators had publicly claimed that they would vote against the treaty for no other reason than that it bore the name of the secretary of state.

A motion by Senator Fessenden of Maine to bar the treaty from further discussion was voted down—yeas 12, nays 29. Fol-

*Senators Cameron of Pennsylvania*
*and Patterson of New Hampshire*
*were members of the Committee*
*on Foreign Relations, which considered*
*the Alaska purchase treaty*

lowing this came the crucial support of Charles Sumner, one of the most forceful orators in the country. The Alaskan Treaty was at the mercy of his influence.

Although originally unenthusiastic about Alaska, and a bitter opponent of President Johnson, Sumner was persuaded by Seward to support the treaty. As a result, he gave a brilliant, almost three-hour-long speech favoring the Alaskan purchase. It was made with only a single sheet of notes before him.

The decision was now up to the Senate.

# Why the Purchase?

To say that the chief reason the United States bought Alaska was William H. Seward is an oversimplification. Thomas Bailey in his article "Why the United States Purchased Alaska" says that such an opinion was stated by a modern historian. No one will deny that Seward was chiefly responsible for the negotiation of the purchase treaty. The overlooked fact is that secretaries of state do not and cannot buy vast tracts of foreign territory. Seward had to secure the approval of the President and his cabinet, of two thirds of the Senate, and of a majority of the House of Representatives.

De Stoeckl's thoughts on why Seward wanted the purchase are interesting. The Russian minister thought that the American secretary of state was not a farsighted statesman and therefore would not see the political and economic importance of Alaska. De Stoeckl was, rather, of the opinion that Seward was interested in the purchase because the secretary hoped that it would bring him once more into popular favor. In order to show the importance of his act, Seward helped to spread reports that Alaska was sold and bought to embarrass Britain. This was done in order to counterbalance the Canadian Confederation, and for other reasons.

Some books also say that Russo-American friendship was the reason that the United States purchased Alaska. This theory is important to consider, since, as we know, the Russian fleet did appear to aid the North during the American Civil War.

However, even at the time, at least a minority of Americans, including Senator Charles Sumner, realized that the Russian naval demonstration might have had ulterior motives. The truth was not uncovered, however, until 1915, when Dr. Frank A. Golder, drawing upon official Russian records, published an article in *The American Historical Review*. Concerning the article, Thomas Bailey writes:

> *The Russo-Polish crisis came to a head in 1863, with a strong possibility of interference by the British and French. If intervention should occur, an armed clash would follow, and the Russian fleet would be bottled up in the Baltic by the British, as it had been during the Crimean War. The Russian Siberian squadron would be set upon jointly by the British and French, who had better telegraphic facilities and who consequently would get word of hostilities first.*
>
> *The objective of the Russian high command was to get its fleets away from these vulnerable mousetraps, base them on neutral ports, and utilize them as individual commerce destroyers, in the manner of the Alabama, to prey on the rich and vulnerable merchant marine of the enemy, especially Great Britain. For such purposes the United States was ideal. San Francisco and New York were well situated for access to shipping lanes; and the Russians, after carefully nurturing American good will all these years, could count upon a hospitable reception. The presence in the United States of these potential raiders would presumably exert pressure on the French, and particularly on the British, to go slowly in the Polish crisis. At all events, when the storm*

*Senator Charles Sumner was an important voice in the fate of the treaty*

*had blown over and the fleets had served their purpose, the commanders were ordered home in 1864.*

It is apparent from these statements that the popular American assumption concerning the mission of the Russian fleet was inaccurate. However, it was long listed as a reason why the United States purchased Alaska.

The Committee on Foreign Affairs published an official report giving its reasons for the purchase. The Congressional Report, published on May 18, 1868, read:

*There were, first the laudable desires of the Pacific Coast to share in the prolific fisheries of the oceans, seas, and rivers of the western world; the refusal of Russia to renew the charter of the Russian American Fur Company in 1866; the friendship of Russia for the United States; the necessity of preventing the transfer by any possible chance, of the northwest coast of America to an unfriendly power; the creation of new industrial interests on the Pacific necessary to the supremacy of our empire on the sea and land; and finally to facilitate and secure the advantages of an unlimited American commerce with the friendly powers of Japan and China.*

# Popular Reaction
# and
# Seward's Campaign

So secretly and rapidly were the treaty negotiations carried
through that few Americans were aware of what was going on.
It was only after the treaty was signed that the secretary of state
gave the news to papers friendly to him. Through them the public learned of the purchase.

Opposition showed itself at once. The American people
called the transaction "a dark deed done in the night"; they could
scarcely believe what had happened. The Alaskan territory
soon became synonymous with such names as "Walrussia,"
"Johnson's Polar Bear Garden," "Frigidia," and "Seward's Ice-
box." *The New York Herald* published this insert: "How to
make both ends meet—buy Patagonia, Mr. Seward." The same
newspaper carried this advertisement:

> *Cash! Cash! Cash! Cash paid for castoff territory. Best
> price given for old Colonies, North or South. Any impov-
> erished monarchs retiring from the colonization business
> may find a good purchaser by addressing W.H.S. [Seward],
> Post Office, Washington, D.C.*

The opposition to ratification appeared so overwhelming to
Charles Sumner that he now asked de Stoeckl to withdraw the
treaty because it had not the least chance of being confirmed. De
Stoeckl replied that it would be dishonorable on the part of the
United States government to withdraw.

Seward, however, did not lose heart. He quickly converted

the disillusioned Charles Sumner to throw himself into the cause of getting the treaty ratified. Then the resourceful secretary of state realized that the greatest opposition came from those who were most ignorant of Alaska's resources, and he concluded that only a vigorous campaign of instruction directed to the people might save the treaty.

Seward was aware that the unexpectedness and suddenness of the transaction, the immensity of the domain involved, and an utter ignorance of its nature and resources had caused a state of bewilderment in the public's mind. He began the campaign by handing to the press a number of letters from influential men who favored the purchase. The secretary also got support from various persons who had visited the territory, such as R. M. Collins, promoter of the Trans-Pacific line. Collins predicted that:

> the fisheries . . . will build up a population and commerce there which, at no distant day, will rival that of Newfoundland and the coast of the Atlantic East of Cape Cod! Furthermore, these fisheries would serve as a nursery for first-class seamen, which in the growing commerce of the Pacific, will be just what we want there in the future, in order to give us the supremacy of the great ocean.

New England sea captains testified as to the value of the territory. An annexation sentiment was also voiced by citizens and officials in California and Washington. They protested that rejecting the treaty would cause great dissatisfaction on the coast, and that losing the territory would create a feeling not only of disappointment but also of injury.

*The great Alaskan wilderness—*
*shooting the rapids on the Yukon*

Seward discovered that the opposition was voicing objections similar to those voiced by the Federalists against the purchase of the Louisiana Territory in 1803. So he sent a clerk to New York to copy passages from the newspapers of that time. These excerpts, which told of the attacks against President Thomas Jefferson, were printed by the daily press of 1867.

This widespread and persevering education campaign did not escape the attention of keen observers. The *New York Herald*, on April 9, 1867, remarked that:

> *the illustrious Premier is working the telegraphs and the Associated Press in the manufacture of public opinion night and day.*

On the same day, the same newspaper gave a vivid description of Seward's lobbying in Congress:

> *Secretary Seward had another diplomatic symposium at his elegant establishment tonight, at which Mr. Sumner is present, with numerous other Senatorial luminaries. Madame Rumor again associates Russian-American icebergs and refrigerated champagne; and, putting this and that together, makes Mr. Seward's dinner bear in some way on the proposed slice of hyperborean territory.*

Seward's successful enlistment of Sumner's support also helped the discreetly launched education campaign. Not only did Sumner's brilliant three-hour speech influence the ratification, but its subsequent publication produced a tremendous reaction from the public. The *Boston Journal* published the speech in full, along with this article:

*An early photograph of the Alaskan settlement of Hoonah*

*This speech, it will be remembered, coming from the chairman of the Committee on Foreign Affairs, and abounding in a mass of pertinent information not otherwise accessible to Senators, exerted a most marked if not decisive, effect. . . . Since then, the rumors of Mr. Sumner's exhaustive treatment of the subject, together with the increasing popular interest . . . , have stimulated a general desire for the publication of the speech, which we are now able to supply. As might be expected, the speech is a monument of comprehensive research, and of skill in the collection and arrangement of facts. It probably comprises about all the information that is known . . . and will prove equally interesting to the student of history, the politician, and the man of business.*

Soon after the appearance of Sumner's speech, copies were purchased in large quantities by Seward, who used it to combat the public's ignorance concerning Alaska. Because of this intensive campaign, the *New York Herald* observed, on April 8, 1867, as did the *Sacramento Union* a day later, that the chances for ratifying the purchase treaty were much better than the week before.

# The Collins Overland
# Telegraph Company

Secretary of State Seward's campaign of instruction concerning Alaska, of which Senator Sumner's speech was an integral part, greatly influenced the Senate's vote on April 9, 1868. The outcome of that vote might have been far different had not a relatively unknown incident given both Seward and Sumner a contemporary and authentic source of knowledge concerning the huge northern territory.

The incident began on July 8, 1865, when a fleet of twenty-four vessels sailed out of San Francisco harbor. Five hundred adventurous young men—surveyors, explorers, and engineers—staffed the decks as the expedition headed northward. The cargo stowed below was rather unusual. In addition to the standard supply of rifles, axes, and ammunition, there were several tons of greenglass insulators and 1,200 miles of iron telegraph wire. This was the telegraph armada setting out to build the Collins Overland Telegraph to unite America and Europe by land, linking New York and Paris by 16,000 miles of pole-strung wire. The American Congress, which at first showed reluctance toward the project, had finally passed Public Act 171, and President Lincoln had signed his name on the document that appropriated $50,000 for the enterprise.

Previous attempts to complete an Atlantic cable from the United States to Europe had failed. (The Russians had already completed three quarters of their 7,000-mile line from St. Petersburg to Amur before the Americans even took to the field.) The Western Union Telegraph Company, inspired by the advice of Perry McDonough Collins, former United States com-

mercial agent at the mouth of the Amur River, Siberia, began in 1864 to consider an overland telegraph line. It was to extend from the eastern shore of Puget Sound, off what is now the state of Washington, through British and Russian territory, and across the Bering Strait and Siberia to St. Petersburg. The plan also included a survey of American territory and the Yukon River. Major Robert Kennicott agreed to become chief of explorations, providing he might be permitted to select a corps of assistants who would collect scientific data from the natural history of the region. The scientific findings were to be divided between the Chicago Academy of Science and the Smithsonian Institution in Washington, D.C.

Major Kennicott was already, at the age of thirty, an exceptional Arctic explorer and one of the leading naturalists of the day. He had organized the Museum of Natural History at Northwestern University when only twenty-two years of age and at twenty-four had explored the Russian American Colony for the Smithsonian. Kennicott was the first to discover that the Yukon emptied not into the Arctic Ocean but into the Pacific. It is no wonder that the Smithsonian recommended Kennicott when the telegraph company began its search for a qualified explorer.

One of the six assistants from the institution selected to accompany Kennicott was Henry M. Bannister, who was to make meteorological observations and collections. He had been stationed at St. Michael's in Russian America.

During the winter of 1865–66, Major Kennicott and three companions traveled to Nulato, a Russian post some five hundred miles up the Yukon River. There he planned to ascend the

*Major Robert Kennicott*
*explored a good deal of Alaska*

stream when the ice melted, and there also he met his untimely death. Robert Kennicott died in the Alaskan wilderness attempting to save a companion who had fallen into the icy waters of the Yukon. The naturalist did not live to hear that the Atlantic cable had been successfully laid, nor did he ever know that the Collins Overland Telegraph Company was destined to be a colossal failure. However, his carefully prepared directions for further explorations were carried out by his associates.

Henry Bannister returned to Washington from the Overland Telegraph Expedition to Russian America. He made his report to the secretary of the Smithsonian Institution two months before the signing of the Alaskan purchase treaty. Bannister was the only person then in Washington who could give an eye-witness account of the conditions in Alaska. Sumner and Seward turned to him for definite information on the proposed purchase. The secretary of state and the senator also took advantage of Bannister's ability to read and speak the Russian language. This especially prepared him to help the senator peruse the Russian literature available in the Smithsonian and congressional libraries. From these sources Bannister collected quite an amount of useful material for the senator. Bannister also said that he saw Sumner several times when the senator was preparing his speech on the annexation of Alaska. At the time Secretary Seward was with Spencer Fullerton Baird, assistant secretary of the Smithsonian Institution.

Sumner's dependence on Bannister's help is realized by this short communication from Baird. In his letter of April 3, 1867, the assistant secretary wrote:

*Spencer Fullerton Baird, assistant*
*secretary of the Smithsonian Institution*

*Dear Mr. Sumner,*

*Have you a copy of the work on the Russian American Fur Company? If so please let me have it and I will ask Bannister to look it over and see if it has anything bearing on the question.*

Kennicott had pioneered much of Bannister's research through his own observations in Alaska. During the brief existence of the Collins Overland Expedition, Kennicott had visited the Russian American colony. As an explorer for the Smithsonian, Kennicott had spent three years on his own expedition. The mission took him through rivers and lakes, from Lake Superior through central British America. He traveled down the Mackenzie River as far as Peal's River, latitude 67°30′, crossing the mountains and descending the Yukon River to Fort Yukon, a Hudson Bay trading post some two hundred miles within the Russian American territory.

*Each year, after Kennicott returned from these expeditions to the Northwest, there appeared in the annual reports of the Smithsonian Institution glowing accounts of the contributions he was making to a knowledge of that region.*

The Smithsonian's report for 1863 states:

*. . . have seen specimens of new or rare forms intended to advance the study of Natural History. The collections of Mr. Kennicott procured in his explorations are of a very valuable character, illustrating the natural history and ethnology of the northwestern portions of the continent of North America.*

When Kennicott returned to Washington from that trip, he brought with him collections of animals and birds, many of them new to science, which he placed in the Smithsonian. He also recorded a journal published in the first volume of the *Transactions of the Chicago Academy of Science* in 1869. The journal was written while he was in Russian America and it included information about the region through which he traveled. Of vital importance were the observations he made on the climate, natural resources, and native languages.

An 1867 Smithsonian report states:

*Indicative of the growing interest in the Smithsonian was the passing of a Senate resolution providing for the printing of 6,000 additional copies of the report of the Board of Regents for the past year ending June 30, 1865. Three thousand of these were for the use of Senators. A similar resolution was passed by the House of Representatives and 3,000 were to be for the use of the Representatives.*

Sumner was greatly dependent upon the testimony of some of the personnel of the Smithsonian and upon the annual reports of the institution for contemporary conditions in Alaska. Secretary of State Seward also made extensive use of the information found in the Smithsonian.

Senator Sumner, in his speech before the Senate on April 9, 1867, mentions his grateful dependence on the expedition sent out by the Russian American Telegraph Company for "authentic evidence with regard to the character of the region, and the great rivers that transverse it."

Also in this speech, he particularly indicated the reliable information contributed in its preparation by Robert Kennicott and Henry M. Bannister. Of Kennicott he states:

*His name will always remind us of courageous enterprise, before which distance and difficulty disappeared. He was*

*not a beginner, when he entered into the service of the Telegraph Company. Already he had visited the Yukon country by the way of the Mackenzie River, and contributed to the Smithsonian Institution important information with regard to its geography and natural history, some of which is found in their Reports. Nature in novel forms was open to him.*

*The Smithsonian Institution, Washington, D.C., founded in 1846 through a bequest of over $500,000 from James Smithson, an Englishman who never visited the United States*

# Vote, Delay,
# and Bribery

Mainly through the campaign of William H. Seward and the speech of Charles Sumner, the United States Senate ratified the treaty for the purchase of Alaska on April 9, 1867, by a vote of 37 to 2. The dissenting votes were cast by William Fessenden and Justin Morrill of New England, perhaps a natural reaction from a section of the country that feared the competition of the Alaskan fisheries.

On May 15, de Stoeckl informed Seward that the treaty had also been ratified by the Russian government.

*Mr. de Stoeckl to Mr. Seward*
*(Telegram)*
*New York, May 15, 1867.*

*William H. Seward:*
    *Just received the following telegram from St. Petersburg: "Treaty Ratified. Bodisco carries it back and leaves imme—Gorchakov."*
    *I shall be in Washington tomorrow.*

                                                        *Stoeckl*

Russia and the United States exchanged ratification of the Alaskan Treaty on June 20, 1867. The only action left to consummate the transaction was the payment of the purchase price.

*A view of what the sale*
*was all about—part of the*
*beautiful Alaska territory*

*Cartoon from the
Johnson impeachment era*

Several American ships were anxious to visit the territory, so, upon Seward's request, the czar opened the territory to American ships even before the $7.2 million was deposited into the imperial treasury.

At Sitka, Alaska, as the Russian flag was lowered and the Stars and Stripes raised, Russian soldiers under a Captain Pestchourev and Americans under Brigadier-General Lovell H. Rousseau fired a salute.

The result of the Senate's approval of the treaty greatly pleased de Stoeckl, Gorchakov, and Alexander II.

> *On one of the minister's accounts of the sale the Emperor wrote "pour tout cela il mérite un 'spasibo' [Thanks] de ma part," and instructed the chancellor . . . to reward him with 25,000 rubles [$18,621], and Bodisco, the secretary of the legation, with 5,000 [$3,724].*

It soon became apparent, however, that there was a movement in the United States House of Representatives to block appropriation of the purchase money. On July 6, 1867, President Johnson sent a message to Congress requesting an appropriation of $7.2 million. Congress adjourned without taking action. That November, Congress reconvened—but for six months its attention was absorbed by the impeachment proceedings against the President. During that period every measure or recommendation of the executive department was scorned by the legislature. This attitude made it highly questionable whether the cession would receive congressional sanction or whether the necessary funds would be requisitioned. The biggest argument that some representatives claimed in their defense was that the House of Representatives should have been consulted beforehand in a matter necessitating an appropriation of money.

The situation proved embarrassing to Secretary of State

Seward, with Alaska already in American possession and Congress having taken no action. However, on March 23, 1868, Seward wrote a note of reassurance to de Stoeckl:

> *On my return from Auburn yesterday, I received from the Honorable Mr. Banks, chairman of the Committee on Foreign Affairs of the House of Representatives, a note . . . in which he says to me in substance that the dispatches of the Associative Press give an erroneous statement of the action of the Committee of Foreign Affairs in regard to the Russian treaty. He further states that it is believed that the approaching trial in the Senate will suspend all public business in the House of Representatives during its progression; that the members of the committee, in this belief, consented informally to pass the subject until the trial should be ended, but he added that it should not be understood as a result of opposition to the bill, but a recognition of the inevitable course of public business. Mr. Banks concludes with the opinion that the Committee will report in favor of the payment and the appropriation will be made by the House of Representatives in exact pursuance of the conditions of the bill. It is hardly necessary to say that the statements thus made by the chairman of the Committee on Foreign Affairs are altogether reliable. I have thought proper to give you this information for the use of your government.*

This note sent by the secretary of state did not alleviate the fears of the Russian minister. He became increasingly worried. Not only were his reputation and the dignity of his country involved but the friendly relations between the two nations were at stake. The case seemed almost hopeless to the Russian minister. This conviction led him to reason that there were two dignified courses to take:

To tell the United States that Russia had done its part, and if the United States was unwilling to pay for Alaska, they could have it without paying.

To send a strong, but courteous note that would touch American pride.

Toward the end of March, 1968, de Stoeckl wired these alternate courses to his home government and awaited instructions. He received a reply from the Russian minister of foreign affairs sanctioned by the czar. It favored the second alternative, fearing that if the first were offered it might be accepted by the Americans.

President Johnson wished to send a special message to Congress. De Stoeckl, however, wished both the President and his secretary of state to remain in the background. As far as the matter was concerned, the Russian minister felt that their pressure on Congress might result in more harm than good.

Nathaniel Prentiss Banks, chairman of the Committee on Foreign Affairs of the House of Representatives, evidently had the situation in hand. On May 18, 1868, the bill appropriating the $7.2 million was reported from the Committee of Foreign Affairs. On July 14 it passed the House by a vote of 113 to 43. It passed the Senate on July 17 and was signed into law on July 27.

De Stoeckl's work in America was completed. The strain to get the appropriation bill passed had left him disgusted with the lawmakers at the Capitol. He pleaded with his foreign office to remove him from Washington, to send him anywhere it pleased. Although discouraged with the United States legislators, Edouard de Stoeckl never changed his high opinion of the American people.

Even with the treaty ratified and the money paid, Secretary Seward was still in the middle of controversy. His amazing success in maneuvering public opinion behind the treaty soon brought charges of bribery against him. On December 14, 1868, the Committee on Public Expenditures investigated allegations that Nathaniel Prentiss Banks, Thaddeus Stevens, and other members of Congress had been bribed. It was also alleged that various newspaper correspondents and proprietors had been bought, and that Seward himself had been well reimbursed for his part in the deal.

The findings of the investigating committee were weak, largely because the Russian delegation refused to comply with the committee's request to furnish data in regard to certain disbursements said to have been made by de Stoeckl.

Seward denied the assertions of bribery and testified that he had spent $500 on his education campaign. He was challenged no further.

It is interesting to note the following reference that Professor W. A. Dunning makes to a document he found among President Johnson's papers. It tells of an incident that the President wrote down upon returning to Washington in early September, 1868. This is the uncorrected memorandum that Dunning found and published:

> *On the sixth Sept. Sunday Mr. Seward and myself rode out some seven or eight miles on the road leading to Masboro Md . . . near place called old fields, we drove out into a shady grove of oak trees—. While there taking some refreshments, in the current of conversation on various subjects, the Secretary asked the question if it ever occurred to*

*Washington, D.C.,*
*around the time of the*
*purchase of Alaska*

*me how few members there were in Congress whose actions were beyond pecuniary influence. I replied that I had never attempted to reduce it to an accurate calculation; but I regretted to confess that there was a much smaller number exempt than at one period of life I had supposed them to be—. He then stated you remember that the appropriations of the seven $ million for the payment of Alaska to the Russian Govt was hung up or brought to a deadlock in the H— of Reps— while the appropriation was thus delayed the Russian minister stated to me that John W. Forney stated to him that he needed $30,000 in gold.*

*That there was no chance of the appropriation passing the House of Reps without certain influence was brought to bear in its favor—. The 30,000 was paid, hence the advocacy of the appropriation in the chronicle—. He also stated that $20,000 was paid to R. J. Walker and F. P. Stanton for their services—. N. P. Banks Chairman of the Committee of Foreign Relations $8,000 and that the incorruptible Thaddeus Stevens received as his "sop" the moderate sum of $10,000—. All these sums were paid by the Russian minister directly and indirectly to the respective parties to secure appropriation of money the govnt had stipulated to pay the Russian Govnt in solemn treaty which had been ratified by both Govnts. . . .*

Professor Dunning did not place much faith in the document's authenticity. He calls it "hearsay in the second degree" because it is Johnson's account of Seward's recital of what de Stoeckl had said. Also the fact that Seward and Johnson had partaken of refreshment—probably liquid—could be a cause to invalidate what was said.

# Afterthoughts

In part of the testimony offered by Spencer Fullerton Baird and Henry Bannister, the following seems to sum up the purchase of Alaska:

> *The annexation was ridiculed at the time but we could testify that the country was worth the price asked. Time has sufficiently proved that we were right and I can safely say that we did not overstate anything. . . .*

Many years later, a story in *The New York Times* on January 29, 1974, stated:

> *Referring to complaints in the United States that wheat had been sold to the Russians at low prices in 1972, Vladimir S. Alkhimov, a Deputy Minister of Foreign Trade stated: "We bought the wheat at market prices. They may have been low, but look at Alaska, which we sold you for $7 million back in 1867. That was cheap, too, but you don't hear us complaining."*

This is not entirely true, according to historian Robert Reynolds, who states in *Outlines of Modern and Recent History of the U.S.A.*, published by the Soviet Academy of Sciences, that the Russians find it difficult to reconcile themselves to the loss of so valuable a possession. "A mere 7.2 million dollars," they wistfully exclaim, was paid for this "huge territory"—one that was shortly discovered to be burgeoning with "rich gold deposits and coal reserves."

Presently, it has been estimated that Alaska's virgin forests alone contain over 350 billion board feet of timber. Minerals

each year produce over $25 million, and Alaska's biggest industry —fisheries—alone has produced a total of more than $2 billion since 1867. All of this and very much more in untapped resources for the bargain price of two cents an acre!

*Modern Alaskans with just one of the land's great riches—the whale*

# A Selected
# Bibliography

Bailey, Thomas A. *America Faces Russia: Russian-American Relations From Early Times to Our Day*. New York: Cornell University Press, 1950.

———. *A Diplomatic History of the American People*. 6th ed. New York: Appleton-Century-Crofts, 1958.

———. "Why the United States Purchased Alaska." *The Pacific Historical Review* 3 (March, 1934).

Depperman, W. H. "Two Cents an Acre." *North American Review* 245 (March, 1938).

Golder, Frank A. "The Purchase of Alaska." *The American Historical Review* 25 (April, 1920).

Hulley, Clarence C. *Alaska: 1741–1953*. Portland, Ore.: Binfords and Mort, 1953.

James, James Alton. *The First Scientific Expedition in Russian America and the Purchase of Alaska*. Evanston, Ill.: Northwestern University Studies in Political Science, no. 4, 1942.

Seward, Frederick W. *Reminiscences of a Wartime Statesman and Diplomat 1830–1915*. New York: G. P. Putnam's Sons, 1916.

Spicer, George W. *The Constitutional Status and Government of Alaska*. Baltimore, Md.: Johns Hopkins Press, 1927.

Sumner, Charles. *Works*. Boston: Lee and Shepard, 1875.

Thomas, Benjamin P. *Russo-American Relations 1815–1867*. Baltimore, Md.: Johns Hopkins Press, 1930.

# Index